SALINA LIBRARY
100 BELMONT STREET
MATTYDALE, NY 13211
315-454-4524

Extreme Sports

SNOWBOARDING

Allan Morey

DiscoverRoo
An Imprint of Pop!
popbooksonline.com

abdobooks.com

Published by Pop!, a division of ABDO, PO Box 398166, Minneapolis, Minnesota 55439. Copyright © 2021 by POP, LLC. International copyrights reserved in all countries. No part of this book may be reproduced in any form without written permission from the publisher. Pop!™ is a trademark and logo of POP, LLC.

Printed in the United States of America, North Mankato, Minnesota.

052020
092020

THIS BOOK CONTAINS RECYCLED MATERIALS

Cover Photo: G-Team-MN
Interior Photos: G-Team-MN; iStockphoto, 5, 6, 7, 8–9, 12, 14, 16, 23, 27, 29, 30; Red Line Editorial, 11; Calle Hesslefors/ullstein bild/Getty Images, 13; Shutterstock Images, 15, 19, 20, 21, 22, 25, 28, 31; Robert F. Bukaty/AP Images, 17

Editor: Brienna Rossiter
Series Designer: Jake Slavik

Library of Congress Control Number: 2019954964
Publisher's Cataloging-in-Publication Data

Names: Morey, Allan, author.
Title: Snowboarding / by Allan Morey
Description: Minneapolis, Minnesota : POP!, 2021 | Series: Extreme sports | Includes online resources and index.
Identifiers: ISBN 9781532167874 (lib. bdg.) | ISBN 9781532168970 (ebook)
Subjects: LCSH: Snowboarding--Juvenile literature. | Snowboarders--Juvenile literature. | Winter sports--Juvenile literature. | Extreme sports--Juvenile literature. | Sports--Juvenile literature.
Classification: DDC 796.046--dc23

WELCOME TO
DiscoverRoo!

Pop open this book and you'll find QR codes loaded with information, so you can learn even more!

Scan this code* and others like it while you read, or visit the website below to make this book pop!

popbooksonline.com/snowboarding

*Scanning QR codes requires a web-enabled smart device with a QR code reader app and a camera.

TABLE OF CONTENTS

CHAPTER 1
At the Terrain Park 4

CHAPTER 2
History 10

CHAPTER 3
Snowboarding Today 18

CHAPTER 4
Snowboard Safety 26

Making Connections 30
Glossary 31
Index 32
Online Resources 32

CHAPTER 1
AT THE TERRAIN PARK

A snowboarder races down a mountain slope. As she picks up speed, she leans left. The edge of her board cuts into the snow, causing her to turn left. Then she

WATCH A VIDEO HERE!

Carving is when a snowboarder turns by tilting the snowboard onto an edge.

leans right. Her board curves back across

the slope.

Soon, she nears a ramp. She shoots up its side and launches off the top. In midair, she bends down to grab her board's edge. Then she begins to spin. She does a half-turn before landing in a puff of snow.

In an Indy grab, a snowboarder reaches between his or her knees to grab the board.

Snowboarders bend their knees before and after going off jumps.

DID YOU KNOW? The name of a spin trick tells how far the snowboarder turns. A half-turn is called a 180. A full spin is a 360.

Jibbing *is a snowboarding term for jumping or sliding on rails or other obstacles.*

Next, a jump sends her up onto a rail. She slides her board along it. Then she hops off the end. The snowboarder flies off a few more jumps. Then she leaves the **terrain park** and continues curving back and forth down the mountain.

CHAPTER 2
HISTORY

Snowboarding got its start in the 1960s. In 1965, Sherman Poppen nailed two skis together. He made a board that could slide on snow. It looked similar to a short surfboard. His wife called it the Snurfer.

LEARN MORE HERE!

This name comes from combining the words *snow* and *surfer*.

BINDINGS

Early snowboards were hard to ride. Nothing kept a rider's feet on the board. In the 1970s, Jake Burton added bindings. These straps hold the rider's feet in place. They give the rider better control. Bindings made it easier for snowboarders to turn and do tricks. As a result, the sport's popularity grew.

This new way of sliding downhill caught on quickly. In the 1970s, several companies began making snowboards.

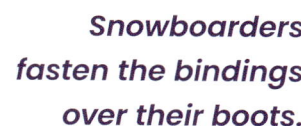

Snowboarders fasten the bindings over their boots.

Throughout the 1970s and 1980s, more and more snowboarders could be seen on ski slopes.

Ski resorts have slopes for people to ride down and places for people to stay.

The National Snow Surfing Championship began in 1982. At this competition, snowboarders raced downhill at a ski resort in Vermont. In 1984, the competition added a **slalom** event. The next year, the championship was renamed the US Open.

In slalom, snowboarders curve back and forth to go around flags.

DID YOU KNOW? Doug Bouton won the first National Snow Surfing Championship. He went nearly 60 miles per hour (97 km/h).

In the mid-1980s, ski resorts began building **halfpipes**. Snowboarders flew up the sides to do tricks. This new style of snowboarding was added to the US Open in 1988.

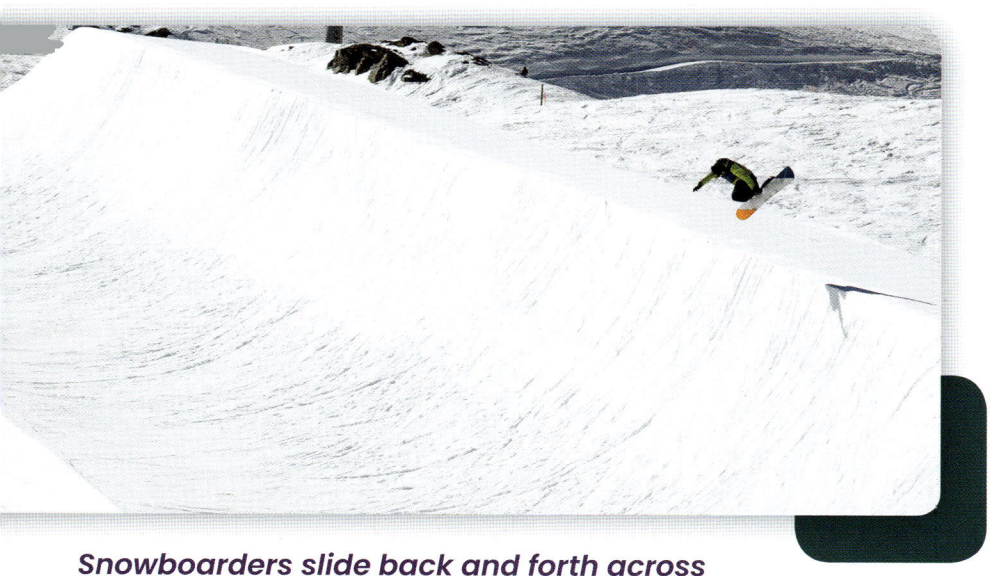

Snowboarders slide back and forth across the halfpipe. They do a trick each time they reach an edge.

Jerry Tucker competes in the US Snowboard Grand Prix in 1996.

Other competitions opened too. Snowboarding was part of the first Winter X Games in 1996. And it became an Olympic sport in 1998.

CHAPTER 3
SNOWBOARDING TODAY

Today, there are snowboarding events and competitions around the world. They feature several different snowboarding styles. **Halfpipe** remains one of the most

LEARN MORE HERE!

popular. But snowboarders also compete in **slalom** and other styles.

Victor Habermacher flies off the halfpipe during the 2012 Youth Olympic Games.

In snowboard cross, small groups race through a series of jumps and turns.

In snowboard cross, four to six snowboarders race down a course. They speed over drops, fly off jumps, and race around **berms**. This event is also known as boardercross.

A superpipe is a halfpipe with tall, straight sides. Riders zoom back and forth doing tricks. They get points for height, difficulty, and style.

JJ Thomas won the superpipe final at the 2010 Winter Dew Tour.

The sides of a superpipe are more than 16 feet (4.9 m) tall.

Big air snowboarders slide down a huge ramp to gain speed before a jump launches them into the air.

In big air snowboarding, riders go off very large jumps. They do spins and flips before landing. And in slopestyle, riders take turns riding through a course. The course has jumps and other **obstacles**. Riders do tricks as they fly over them.

Each slopestyle course has three to four jumps plus a few other obstacles.

SUPERSTAR CHLOE KIM

- Chloe Kim began snowboarding when she was four years old. She started competing at age six.

- Her first major competition was the 2014 Winter X Games. She won silver in the superpipe.

- Kim won gold in this event in 2015 and 2016, and she got bronze in 2017.

- Kim competed in the halfpipe at the 2018 Winter Olympics. She won a gold medal.

Chloe Kim was just 17 years old when she won gold at the 2018 Winter Olympics.

- Later that year, Kim won the ESPY Award for Best Female Athlete.

- In addition to snowboarding, Kim enjoys skateboarding and playing guitar.

Chapter 4
Snowboard Safety

While doing tricks and **getting air**, snowboarders can crash or fall. Wearing the right gear can help prevent injuries. Helmets and goggles protect the head.

Complete an activity here!

Goggles help shield a snowboarder's eyes from the glare of the sun on the snow.

Pads protect the elbows, hips, and knees.

Snowboarders wear wrist guards too.

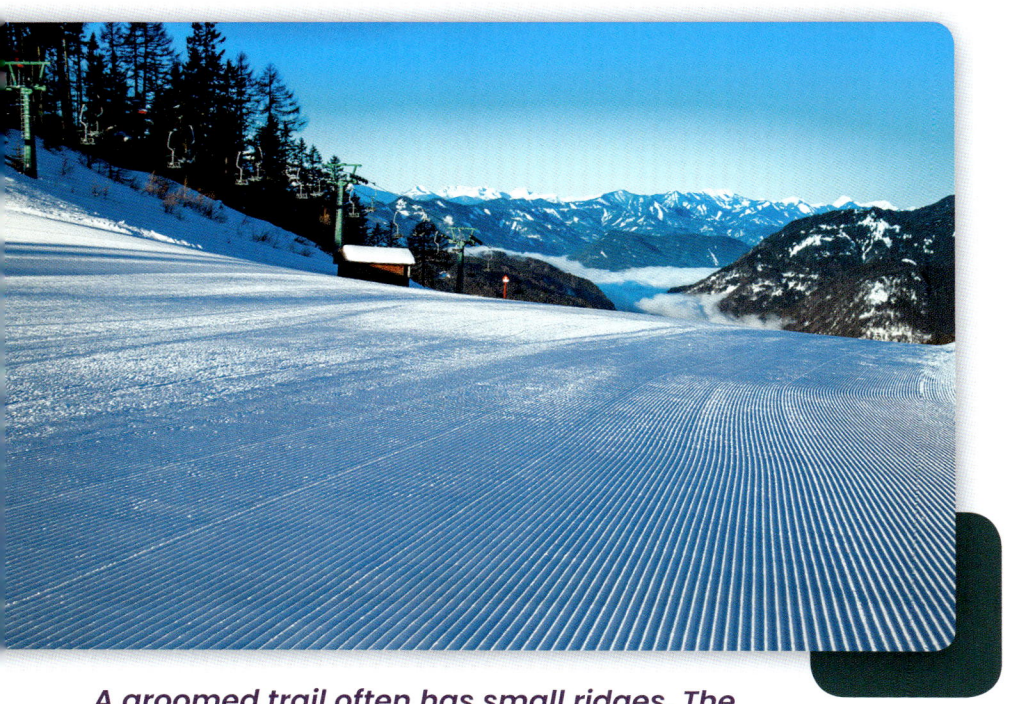

A groomed trail often has small ridges. The ridges help create a smooth, even ride.

Snowboarders also follow safety rules. They never snowboard alone. And they stay on **groomed** trails. If they went off a trail, they could get lost. Or they might hit a tree or rock.

Snowboarders should ride at a comfortable speed. If they go too fast, they can crash.

To stay safe, snowboarders choose slopes that are not too difficult or steep.

DID YOU KNOW? In 2015, Edmond Plawczyk set a world record for snowboard speed. He went 126 miles per hour (203 km/h).

MAKING CONNECTIONS

TEXT-TO-SELF

If you could go snowboarding, would you rather race downhill or ride a halfpipe? Why?

TEXT-TO-TEXT

Have you read about other sports that are part of the Winter Olympics? What sports were they?

TEXT-TO-WORLD

Snowboarding is a way to stay active and healthy. What else can people do to get exercise?

GLOSSARY

berm – a raised side at the corner of a turn.

get air – to lift off the ground, such as by going off a jump or ramp.

groomed – when a trail is prepared for use by smoothing or packing down the snow.

halfpipe – a U-shaped ramp. Athletes move up and down the ramp's sides to do tricks.

obstacle – something that blocks the way.

slalom – a downhill course where athletes zigzag between flags or other obstacles.

terrain park – an area with ramps, rails, and other obstacles people can use to do tricks.

INDEX

big air snowboarding, 23

bindings, 12

competitions, 14–15, 17, 18–19, 24

halfpipe, 16, 18, 20, 24

jumps, 9, 20, 23

slalom, 14, 19

slopestyle, 23

snowboard cross, 20

Snurfer, 10–11

superpipe, 20–21, 24

tricks, 7, 12, 16, 21, 23, 26

ONLINE RESOURCES
popbooksonline.com

Scan this code* and others like it while you read, or visit the website below to make this book pop!

popbooksonline.com/snowboarding

*Scanning QR codes requires a web-enabled smart device with a QR code reader app and a camera.